Mom —
thought you mite
like this gem...

From The Land Of Marmite With Love

,

written by

Agata Palmer

= Fellow Musician
+ a PPM member

with ♡

Robin X

X.

In loving memory of my mother, Mameńka

My thanks to the many beautiful people who have contributed to this work and to Exiled Writers Ink and The Arts Council, England for this transformative project –

Luke, for his loving support.

My poetry mentor, Aviva Dautch, who both inspired and guided me patiently throughout.

The many people who have inspired me over the years: Halina, Florence, Pam, Vicky, Deasy, Yvonne, Ella, Daniella, Bożenka, Denise, Fiona, Jane, Mariusz, Joanna and I could go on, as I've been lucky to meet many wonderful souls.

My sons, for teaching me about love and detachment and for our shared journeys, including the epic train trip, which re-ignited my passion for writing.

My Polish family – you are each a precious part of me and contributed to who I am today.

My zen dog, Cocoa, for being my steady companion for the past 10 years, providing an abundance of canine love and simple joy, especially through lockdown.

I am grateful to the editors of the following publications in which two of these poems appear: 'Decluttering' published in *Alba:A Journal Of Short Poetry* (Winter 2020) and 'Black Arches Moth' in *Beyond Words* (Spring 2021).

'Poets can touch hearts and minds; they can translate trauma into something people can face. [...] That's why I write poetry. Poems are empathy machines.'   **Roger Robinson**

CONTENTS

Migration

On returning, the scent of mum's home
makes me weak at the knees with relief.
My longing is satisfied by her arms and
a bouquet of beeswax, face cream, perfume,
pâté, apple-pie and cheesecake cooling.
Ah, and her hands, silky soft and tender.
How do we make up for the time apart?

The last days before the flight back
we get pensive, irritable, dart tearful glances.
I weep when the plane peels me off my homeland –
this always used to embarrass my sons.
By the time we reach the clouds, re-booting starts:
my psyche re-framing all the reasons
why I manage to live and work there.

Now, back in the land of green hills and marmite,
this quaint island with sweet, thatched cottages,
this country where I grew into an adult,
where our friends and my sons' roots are,
I've come to love it and feel at home here.
It has loved me back into a hybrid me,
which wouldn't have existed otherwise.

Home from home.

Home away from home.

Grateful for both.

Torn between the two.

The Japanese Teapot

Dad's grave needs weeding.
Do you approve of the choice of tombstone?
I don't have an answer,
but it matters very much to Mami.

I caress the delicate curves
of the Japanese teapot:
it's incredible that it journeyed
through war in Grandma's suitcase.

The aroma of aftershave
engulfs me in my brother's hugs –
feeling so safe and dear
closes the gap of no phone calls.

My sister's wide-open heart and home
are always are there for me.
Seeing the family age
in annual instalments is cruel,

offset by the leaps of development
of the young cousins.
Special occasions gone unshared
make us tongue-tied and awkward,

then chatty again. It takes days
to get used to each other,
until it's like I never left –
my other life seems surreal.

Venetian Mirror

In Polish, a Venetian Mirror is a one-way mirror

No matter how integrated you seem
moments will ambush you, when it feels like
looking through glass: people can see in,
but inner shadows will keep you captive
with sticky layers of separateness.

Decluttering

I had this bitter-sweet moment with mountains
of shredded paper, of all things!

An immense critical mass of monochrome
processed tree cellulose,

of previous professions, past diaries, events,
outdated love letters.

There it was, tangible and so last century.
A stack taller than me.

A tower of paper certainty that there is now
more past than future in my life.

The Shape Of An Animal

Seemingly benign, sleek,
smiling in appearance,
hidden from daylight,

it'll surface unexpectedly, usually
at night, to rip your heart open
with its small but effective claws.

You won't be able to see it
or predict its reappearance,
yet it leaves no ground unturned.

Your entire being is a map:
a network of tunnels devoted
to your past and future losses.

Hurricane Barbara

Listen. This hurricane, your namesake,
bashing at the window, shaking its frame,

tearing at fences, showing how bendy
those birches must be to withstand the rage.

This is how your soul must feel, longing
to be free from your paralysed body.

I am here to tell you that your love will remain,
enough to flow through several generations.

Let nothing hold you back. Not even me.
We will do the remembering from now on.

My Queen Of Meadows

She'd make a flower posy for every table,
unstoppable in her beautification zeal.
Being in a desert wouldn't undermine her:
a poet in the kitchen, stylist in fashion,
the encyclopaedias on a daily menu.
She made still-life of daisies and white dead-nettles,
a fan of tulips, my mum, my queen of meadows.
She would stand tall in her slight frame
with integrity, grace, always. A birch, flexing
through history, we knew she was oak at the core.

The Memory Card

Many full moons after the cremation
I needed to use my mum's camera.
When viewing the yet unseen photographs
I was sent reeling into the extremes
of curious excitement and intense grief.
A belated comment from the Beyond
about one languid, sunny afternoon.
An octogenarian – still curious enough
to look under the surface of objects
to find solace from her dense solitude:
flowers from grandchildren, leafy shadows,
objects that had lived through the war with her.
Our calls often ended with a laugh:
Trzeba nad tym popracować, moja Kropelko.

Note: Translation from the Polish: 'It takes some work, my Droplet'

One Flower

You can't have dawn without the sun, a birthday
without a birth-giver, therefore, let me speak straight
about Mother's Day, once and for all.

It's my celebration with you of our lifetimes together,
the sinusoid of becoming who we have grown to be,
with many things to keep and some things

best forgotten, frankly. You fed on rebellion
to power your launch out of our nest. So what?
– you did the best you could – we've each made

teenage blunders. All I need from you is a special flower
twice a year: on Mothering Sunday and 26th May,
the Polish way, as this keeps the branches

of our ancestral tree in leaf. Chosen by you as a symbol,
not a bouquet bought online, but the tribal code
to acknowledge our bond in flesh and blood.

.

Dzień Dziecka

Lit. International Children's Day, celebrated in Poland like Mother's Day

Sometimes silence is simply more eloquent.
This Dzień Dziecka, I tell you with my eyes
how much you mean to me, how proud I am,
how you matter, your whole experience.

You are each on your own hero's journey.
I salute you from where I see you now.
Treasure what you learn, and you *will* know –
in hindsight – how it was all meant to be.

Family Dynamics

1   The dance of need and its fulfilment
2   Mouth-watering familiarity
3   Laying down the textures of shared history
4   The nakedness of knowing each other's stories and faults
5   Easy laughter, easy friction
6   The arrhythmia of conflicting expectations
7   A cacophony of past misunderstandings
8   The bullets in the haystacks of the soul
9   Habits repeated, habits resented, habits treasured
10 *Habimus familium vivat* – how lucky!

Acquitted

The same eyes. The blueness of *forget-me-nots*,
once trustworthy, now a metallic challenge.
The same hands that steadied me, that caressed
our baby's hairy back, now circle my neck,
pressing terror into my throbbing artery.

Our toddler watching and shouting:
Stop fighting! the echoes bouncing around
our terracotta bedroom. He has my mouth.
The same lips that colonised the wilderness
of our shared passions, now lying under oath.

Guilty

Finalising the divorce petition on Valentine's Day
was a coincidence. *Sorry* won't change it now.
In signing it, I pleaded guilty to a crime.
According to my own Book of Law and Fairness,
page five clearly states that ceasing to love you
was against my ethics, against humanity,
against the vows I meant earnestly at the time.
It's punishable by the same happening to me.

Sleep

The privilege of safety,
an ultimate reprieve from all
that otherwise could bother you,
deep drifting into letting go,

your unconscious mind spinning dreams –
the captain of your night crossings,
like a dog fetching past events
and mixing them up with symbols.

Toiling to unravel your knots,
it offers you resolutions
to all aspects of your life: served
in frames of unremembered dreams.

Silence

In our times dominated by words –
texts, e-mails, slogans, blogs, opinions,
causes, allegations, investigations –

I wish to sprinkle Silence upon you,
wrap us up in its deep, soft folds.
Can you taste its vast landscapes?

In Defence Of Literary Language

Some words swoon their necks and sing their vowels
with full roundedness and beauty, while others caw,
missing the note and tone, falling limp on my eardrum.

When boundaries of strong consonants give rhythm,
the start and finish of words' meanings are splendid
like Atlas, holding up the structure with athletic vigour.

I wish to defend literary language. Without it, guides
to pronunciation would be void, dictionaries impure,
our traditions lost and dialect left forever unbalanced.

Dialect

Words of the same ilk flock together
for better or weaker, tweet and trill.
Tribes of the same twang, they gather
chirping their chitter-chatter, cawing,
clawing at straws, until dialect is hatched.

Mind The Gap

You lef– ... where the letter 't' should have been,
it gawps, lingers – a linguistic faux pas.
Your language is scrawny, a blunt scalpel
for castrating words of their potential –
missing the structure, a porridge of sounds.
Why do you rape and pillage your own tongue?

The Guest

A need for writing arises in me
like an unexpected guest
knocking on my door when
I'm enjoying my own company.
After my initial panic, I hide
empty chocolate wrappers
and, with suspicion, see who it is.

Are you here for me? Why now?
Her smile fades under the weight
of my mistrust. We sit
and taste silence together.
Slowly, my hostility melts.
I make her a cup of tea,
walk her around, tell her everything –

about my dog, my children,
my hatchling sculptures. We frame
passing time into observations,
add our marks to the landscape
of collective memories,
just in case I dissolve
into nothingness all too soon.

Silkworm Moth

Have you seen a real silkworm moth up close?
A teddy bear with combs for eyelashes,
she swans in white feathers like a flapper,
ready to break into a Charleston step.

How unsuitable for a farming slave.
To obtain a single kilo of silk, it takes
almost seven thousand worms being killed,
boiled or gassed, depending on the method.

Black Arches Moth

All you'll glimpse will be
the cassock of my wings:
priestess of darkness,
keeper of shadows.
It's how I serve my purpose.
I am the bringer of loss.
I didn't ask for it
but there goes another.

You aren't the only one
pleading *Why me?*
Haven't you noticed
how urgently I long
to follow the light,
until death, just like you.

Prominent Moth

You're like a movie star
from the era of silent films –
glamour in shades of grayscale,
wearing patterned lace with
a furry trim and staccato heels.
I almost expect you to light up
a cigarette in a long holder
and blow smoke playfully

into my eyes. Then, sipping a
highball held in a gloved tentacle,
you tell me all the secrets
of others, overheard in the privacy
of candlelight – you indiscreet
Greta Garbo of the insect world.

Bogong Moth

Like that Australian moth
I nested in my safe cocoon,
a poem, the necessary womb-sack

where – on my own terms –
I incubated myself
into a resilient traveller.